KEEPING MINIBEASTS

GRASSHOPPERS
AND
CRICKETS

© 1991 Franklin Watts

Franklin Watts, Inc.
387 Park Avenue South
New York, N.Y. 10016

Library of Congress Cataloging-in-Publication Data

Watts, Barrie.
    Grasshoppers and crickets / Barrie Watts.
        p.   cm. — (Keeping minibeasts)
    Includes index.
    Summary: Describes where to find grasshoppers and crickets and how
to keep them as pets, feed them, and breed them.
    ISBN: 0-531-14161-6 (lib.) / ISBN: 0-531-15618-4 (pbk.)
    1. Grasshoppers as pets—Juvenile literature.   2. Crickets as
pets—Juvenile literature.   3. Grasshoppers—Juvenile literature.
4. Crickets—Juvenile literature.   [1. Grasshoppers as pets.
2. Crickets as pets.   I. Title.   II. Series.
SF459.G7W37 1991
638'.5726—dc20   90-45996
                                                    CIP AC

Editor: Hazel Poole
Design: K and Co
Consultant: Michael Chinery

Printed in Italy

KEEPING MINIBEASTS

GRASSHOPPERS
AND
CRICKETS

CONTENTS

Franklin Watts
New York ● London ● Toronto ● Sydney

Grasshoppers and crickets are small green or brown insects that can be found in grasses and low shrubs. They both have two large eyes and long, powerful back legs used for jumping great distances. Some of them have wings. Both are

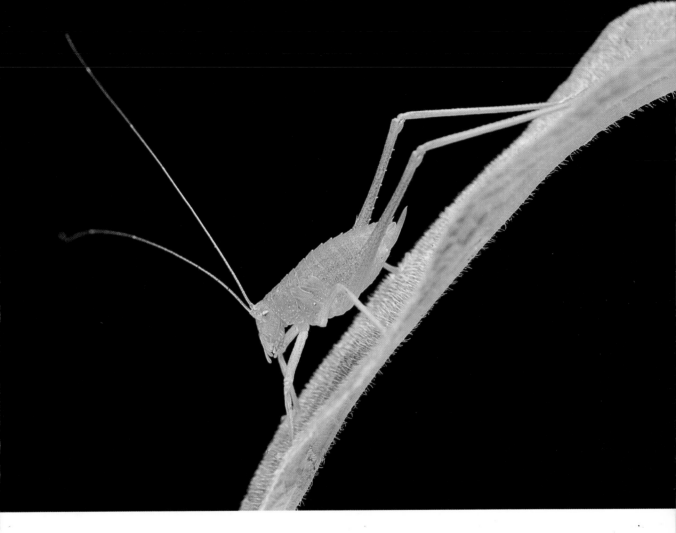

easily found when making their mating calls.
Crickets do this by rubbing their two forewings
together to make a chirping sound.
Grasshoppers rub their back legs against their
forewings, creating a slightly different sound.

One difference between grasshoppers and crickets is the size of their antennae. Grasshoppers have short, thick antennae but a cricket's antennae are long and slender.

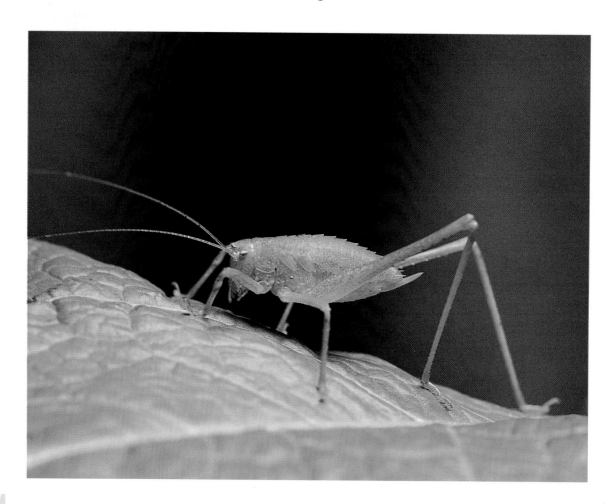

Locusts are a type of grasshopper. They sometimes form huge swarms and cause great damage to crops.

Crickets and grasshoppers can be found in all types of habitat from dry fields and wet marshes to hot deserts. Grasshoppers are usually active during the day and can be found in grassy areas such as fields. There are several groups of crickets. Some live in houses and in burrows underground, but the most common ones are field crickets which can often be found in hedges and are generally active in the evening.

The ideal way to collect grasshoppers is to use a butterfly net. Choose a hot, sunny day and locate the insects by listening for their mating calls.

Collect crickets by encouraging them into a small glass jar as a net would get entangled on bushes and thorny shrubs.

Until you get home, keep your catch temporarily in ice cream containers or jars with airholes in the lids. Make sure you put some grass and leaves in as well so they have something to eat.

If you intend on keeping the insects for a long time to study them, make a proper cage for them. If you provide the correct conditions, the male insects will produce their mating songs.

Setting up a cage

To keep your insects, you will need a large plastic pet cage or aquarium with a lid, some paper towels, leaves and twigs. Line the bottom of the cage with the paper towels as this can

easily be changed when dirty. Put some soil, twigs and leaves in the cage so the insects have shelter and something to climb. Keep the cage on a bright windowsill, but out of direct sunlight and away from radiators.

Field crickets and grasshoppers mostly feed on green vegetation. Grass, leaves, flowers and fruit will give them all they need to eat. Small field crickets, or katydids, also need aphids to

eat, and larger ones need to eat small
grasshoppers or similar insects from time to
time. Only put a small amount in the cage each
day and remove any old food.

Locusts are a type of grasshopper, but very destructive. For this reason, you should not attempt to raise them. They travel in swarms and eat many food crops. They will eat such foods as oats and apples, but also grass.

Locusts breed in dry, sandy areas when temperatures are warm. The female will lay her eggs by pushing the rear of her body into it. The eggs are laid in a long, thin capsule which can contain as many as 100 eggs.

Life cycle

Eggs laid in the spring will hatch in the fall. The tiny hatchling locust nymphs, called hoppers, crawl through the capsule to the sand surface. At this stage they look like miniature adults, but are only as long as a grain of rice.

As they grow, they change their skins, or molt, and also their color. They do this at least four or five times before they reach adult size and maturity.

When you have finished studying your crickets and grasshoppers, let them go. Choose a spot that gives them good cover and food to eat. Do not release any species that are foreign to the area. These could multiply and be a pest to farmers and gardeners. If you can, return occasionally and see if your pets have survived – or multiplied.

There are over 18,000 species of grasshopper and 4,000 species of cricket throughout the world.

Mole crickets have powerful front legs which they use for burrowing. The female crickets spend a great deal of time underground laying their eggs and tending their young nymphs.

Camel crickets usually do not have wings. They often live in greenhouses and feed on aphids and other small insect pests.

A female grasshopper is able to extend her body to almost three times its length in order to lay her eggs in deep sand.

Index